EZEKIEL

Visions of God's Glory

10 STUDIES FOR INDIVIDUALS OR GROUPS

DOUGLAS CONNELLY

An imprint of InterVarsity Press
Downers Grove, Illinois

InterVarsity Press
P.O. Box 1400, Downers Grove, IL 60515-1426
ivpress.com
email@ivpress.com

InterVarsity Press® is the book-publishing division of InterVarsity Christian Fellowship/USA®, a movement of students and faculty active on campus at hundreds of universities, colleges, and schools of nursing in the United States of America, and a member movement of the International Fellowship of Evangelical Students. For information about local and regional activities, visit intervarsity.org.

Cover design: Cindy Kiple
Interior design: Jeanna Wiggins
Image: rocky desert landscape: © Kristian Bell / Moment Collection / Getty Images

ISBN 978-0-8308-3117-3 (print)
ISBN 978-0-8308-6437-9 (digital)

Printed in the United States of America ♾

InterVarsity Press is committed to ecological stewardship and to the conservation of natural resources in all our operations. This book was printed using sustainably sourced paper.

P 18 17 16 15 14 13 12 11 10 9 8 7 6 5 4
Y 35 34 33 32 31 30 29 28 27 26 25

CONTENTS

GETTING THE MOST OUT OF *EZEKIEL*

Ezekiel was a fascinating man who wrote a wonderful book filled with strange and powerful visions. At first glance, Ezekiel seems a little eccentric, but getting to know him is worth the effort. Ezekiel, perhaps more than any other biblical prophet, wanted to know God—and God revealed himself to this prophet in mysterious and mighty ways. You will catch something of the awesome character of God in this book. You will see God in his transcendent glory like in no other part of the Bible. You will come away stunned—and changed by—God's majesty.

THE DAYS OF EZEKIEL

Ezekiel was born in the land of Judah to a family of priests. At the age of twenty he began the ten-year training period required of those who stood before the Lord as intercessors for God's people. But his graduation from the program never came. In 597 BC, when Ezekiel was twenty five years old, he, along with many others, was taken as an exile to Babylon. Over his shoulder he caught a last glimpse of the magnificent Jerusalem temple as he began the seven-hundred-mile walk to a foreign city.

When Ezekiel and the other captives arrived in Babylon, they were settled in an area south of the city on an irrigation canal called the Kebar River. Five years later, when Ezekiel was thirty years old, God called him to be a prophet. He would never serve as a priest in the temple but would speak God's truth to God's people living in exile.

EZEKIEL'S MESSAGE TODAY

Ezekiel's ancient words still speak to us! We too live as foreigners, exiles in a hostile land. Our citizenship as Christians is in heaven. We are part of a kingdom that is not of this world. So how do we survive in a place where we are not welcomed? By keeping our eyes on the God who has called us out of darkness and into his light. We survive by seeing above and beyond the chaos and turmoil of our world into the realm where a sovereign God rules in majesty and power. Ezekiel will help us see the spiritual realm. Though its mysteries are hard to comprehend, we will be greatly helped and comforted by a deeper understanding of and a greater trust in the God who rules over all. So strengthen your heart and pull out your courage as we go on a spiritual journey to places we have never been before.

SUGGESTIONS FOR INDIVIDUAL STUDY

1. As you begin each study, pray that God will speak to you through his Word.

2. Read the introduction to the study and respond to the personal reflection question or exercise. This is designed to help you focus on God and on the theme of the study.

3. Each study deals with a particular passage so that you can delve into the author's meaning in that context. Read and re-read the passage to be studied. The questions are written using the language of the New International Version, so you may wish to use that version of the Bible. The New Revised Standard Version is also recommended.

4. This is an inductive Bible study, designed to help you discover for yourself what Scripture is saying. The study includes three types of questions. Observation questions ask about the basic facts: who, what, when, where, and how. Interpretation questions delve into the meaning of the passage. Application questions help you discover the implications of the text for growing in Christ. These three keys unlock the treasures of Scripture.

Write your answers to the questions in the spaces provided or in a personal journal. Writing can bring clarity and deeper understanding of yourself and of God's Word.

5. It might be good to have a Bible dictionary handy. Use it to look up any unfamiliar words, names, or places.

6. Use the prayer suggestion to guide you in thanking God for what you have learned and to pray about the applications that have come to mind.

7. You may want to go on to the suggestion under "Now or Later," or you may want to use that idea for your next study.

SUGGESTIONS FOR MEMBERS OF A GROUP STUDY

1. Come to the study prepared. Follow the suggestions for individual study mentioned above. You will find that careful preparation will greatly enrich your time spent in group discussion.

2. Be willing to participate in the discussion. The leader of your group will not be lecturing. Instead, he or she will be encouraging the members of the group to discuss what they have learned. The leader will be asking the questions that are found in this guide.

3. Stick to the topic being discussed. Your answers should be based on the verses that are the focus of the discussion and not on outside authorities such as commentaries or speakers. These studies focus on a particular passage of Scripture. Only rarely should you refer to other portions of the Bible. This allows for everyone to participate in in-depth study on equal ground.

4. Be sensitive to the other members of the group. Listen attentively when they describe what they have learned. You may be surprised by their insights! Each question assumes a variety of answers. Many questions do not have "right" answers, particularly questions that aim at meaning or application. Instead the questions push us to explore the passage more thoroughly.

When possible, link what you say to the comments of others. Also, be affirming whenever you can. This will encourage some of the more hesitant members of the group to participate.

5. Be careful not to dominate the discussion. We are sometimes so eager to express our thoughts that we leave too little opportunity for others to respond. By all means participate! But allow others to also.

6. Expect God to teach you through the passage being discussed and through the other members of the group. Pray that you will have an enjoyable and profitable time together, but also that as a result of the study you will find ways that you can take action individually or as a group.

7. Remember that anything said in the group is considered confidential and should not be discussed outside the group unless specific permission is given to do so.

8. If you are the group leader, you will find additional suggestions at the back of the guide.

ONE

APPROACHING THE GOD OF GLORY

Ezekiel 1:1-28

After a discussion about who God is, my perceptive little grandson asked me, "Have you ever seen God?" "Well," I responded, "no, not directly." He wasn't done with the questions, however. "What would you do if you saw God? Would you just talk to him or shake his hand?"

"No," I said, "I think I would fall down." Then I turned the question around. "What would *you* do if you saw God?" "I think," he said, "I would sing him a song!"

Most of us would like to have an encounter with God that would change our lives or calm our hearts, but I'm not sure we are ready to face the awesome majesty of the Lord Almighty.

Group Discussion. Describe a time when you felt far from God. What was the situation, and how did you find your way back to the Lord?

Personal Reflection. Can you remember a time when God captured you, when God spoke into your life in some deep, abiding way? Write down everything you can remember about that encounter with God.

The book of Ezekiel opens with a large group of Israelites living in exile in Babylon. They had been separated from their homeland and their temple for five long years. Among the exiles was a young priest named "God strengthens" or Ezekiel. He was just thirty years old, the age when priests began their ministry in the temple. But for Ezekiel there was no temple to serve in.

On this ordinary day, seven hundred miles from home, God met Ezekiel in a powerful vision. Ezekiel saw the holy God of Israel arrive on his chariot throne—and it changed Ezekiel forever. *Read Ezekiel 1:1-28.*

1. As you review the chapter, which parts of this vision can you visualize and at least partly understand?

2. Which parts of Ezekiel's vision seem weird or difficult?

3. Why did God come to Ezekiel in exile rather than waiting for Ezekiel to return to the temple in Jerusalem?

4. Ezekiel's record devotes a lot of space to the four living creatures. What are these beings, and how would you describe their following features?

- Form:
- Faces:
- Wings:
- Appearance:

5. Next, Ezekiel focuses on the wheels (vv. 15-21). What impresses you about the character and nature of God from Ezekiel's depiction of the wheels?

6. What does Ezekiel hear as he watches this vision unfold (vv. 24, 28)?

7. How does God normally speak into your life?

8. The final feature of Ezekiel's vision is the vault or expanse above the creatures' wings and the one who sat on the throne. How does Ezekiel respond to "the appearance of the likeness of the glory of the LORD" (v. 28)?

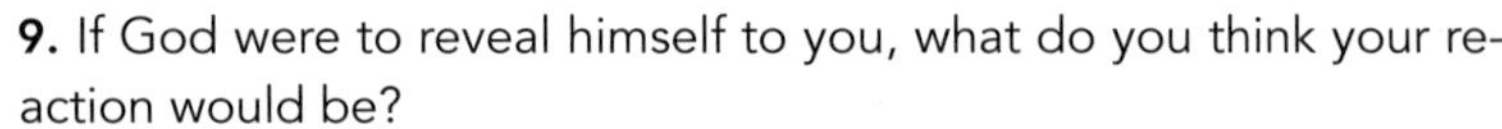

9. If God were to reveal himself to you, what do you think your reaction would be?

10. With Ezekiel 1 in mind, what do you think God most wants you to understand about him?

11. God obviously had Ezekiel's attention. What does God have to do to get you to pay attention to him?

Give God praise for the aspect of his character that impresses you most in this vision. Bow, kneel, or even fall before the Lord in worship. Then listen for his voice.

NOW OR LATER

The prophet Isaiah had a vision of the Lord seated in the temple. Read Isaiah 6:1-5. What similarities do you find between Isaiah's vision and Ezekiel's vision?

What are the differences?

How does Isaiah respond to the Lord's awesome presence?

TWO

THE PREPARATION OF A PROPHET

Ezekiel 2:1–3:15

For **several years** I was an adjunct instructor for a Christian university. I taught a class that introduced students to the Bible and the basic truths of the Christian faith. Every student in every degree program had to take this class. Most of the students were open and even excited about the class, but occasionally a student protested. I got pretty good at spotting objecting students quickly. They would meet me at the classroom door or sit with their arms folded and would say, "Why do I have to take this course? I'm a nursing student (or I'm pursuing a business major). What's the point of a class on the Bible?"

Group Discussion. Have you ever had to lead or teach people who were not interested in what you had to say? Tell the group what you tried to do to break through to them.

Personal Reflection. How do you tend to respond to instruction or information you think is uninteresting or irrelevant to you? Do you sometimes have that same response to God's message?

Ezekiel had been groomed to become a priest in Israel's temple, but that was no longer a possibility. So, God called Ezekiel as a prophet, as a spokesperson for himself, to a stubborn people. *Read Ezekiel 2:1-8.*

1. Who was Ezekiel's audience, and how does God describe them?

2. God uses the word *rebellious* five times to characterize Israel, and he adds the word *rebelled* so no one will miss the point. If God described you six times with one word, what would that word be and why?

3. Who has God placed in your life that needs to hear God's message? What is your "audience" like?

4. Are you challenged or frightened to be sent to your audience? Why?

5. *Read Ezekiel 2:9–3:15.* What does the scroll God gives to Ezekiel represent?

6. Why does God command Ezekiel to eat the scroll, and why is it sweet to him (vv. 3:1-3, 10)?

7. How can we absorb God's Word in our hearts and lives?

8. The people of Judah were not willing to listen to Ezekiel because they were not willing to listen to God (Ezekiel 3:7). Is this still a problem among those of us who claim to follow Jesus? Why?

9. What might leaders, pastors, and teachers be tempted to do in order to gather a larger audience?

10. What resources does God give Ezekiel to help him remain faithful in the face of opposition (Ezekiel 2:2; 3:4; 3:8-9)?

11. Ezekiel is first told to hear, then to become convinced, and then to tell. Where are you in that process?

12. What is keeping you from taking the next step?

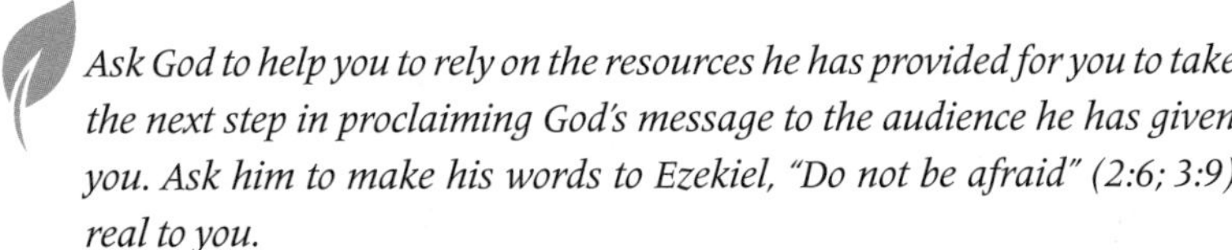

Ask God to help you to rely on the resources he has provided for you to take the next step in proclaiming God's message to the audience he has given you. Ask him to make his words to Ezekiel, "Do not be afraid" (2:6; 3:9), real to you.

NOW OR LATER

The command Ezekiel heard as a prophet has been given to all believers in Colossians 3:16: "Let the message of Christ dwell among you richly as you teach and admonish one another with all wisdom." How can you be sure that you are responding obediently to all that God is saying to you in his Word?

What are some steps you can take to allow the message of Christ to dwell and settle into your mind and heart and life?

THREE

WITNESSING GOD'S JUDGMENT

Ezekiel 5:1-17

The woman who came to the front of the church after the worship service was seeking spiritual help and physical healing. The pastor and a few leaders gathered around her to pray. Suddenly, in his spirit the pastor sensed the Lord's voice telling him to do something he had never done before. "Blow into her face," the Spirit seemed to say.

My pastor friend hesitated just long enough to confirm that it was God's voice he heard. He told the woman that he perceived God was telling him to do something a little unusual, and then he proceeded to blow gently into the woman's face. As he did, tears began to flow from the woman's eyes. She told him later that when he blew across her face, her body and being were flooded with a deep sense of God's love for her.

Group Discussion. Do you think the pastor really heard God's voice, or was it some other influence? How would you have responded if you had been the pastor? If you had been the woman?

Personal Reflection. Have you ever sensed a prompting from God to do something unusual like give money to a stranger or pray for someone you hadn't been thinking about? How did you respond to his direction?

God came to Ezekiel one day and told him to act out a scene that would catch the exiles in Babylon totally off guard. They believed God would deliver them from captivity and return them to Jerusalem.

Ezekiel, however, would show them another scenario—one in which Jerusalem is destroyed and the people living there are massacred. The message of judgment begins with a haircut! *Read Ezekiel 5:1-17.*

1. Describe what Ezekiel was told to do with the hair he shaved from his head and beard (vv. 1-4).

2. What do the hairs represent (v. 12)?

3. What does Ezekiel's action with each portion of his hair symbolize?

- One-third burned:
- One-third slashed with sword:
- One-third blown in the wind:
- A few hairs hidden in Ezekiel's robe:
- A few of the hidden hairs burned:

4. Does God provide any avenue of deliverance from his judgment?

5. In verses 5-11 God tells the people why he will bring such consuming judgment on the inhabitants of Jerusalem. What are his specific complaints against them?

6. Punishment is directed against all those living in Jerusalem. Do you think every person had committed these sins?

7. Does it seem just and fair that everyone is punished?

8. Does God still bring his judgment on his people in the same way? How is it different today?

9. What actions or descriptions of God in verses 14-17 are most disturbing to you?

10. Those of us living under the new covenant no longer face God's wrath against sin. God's wrath was poured out fully on Jesus on the cross, and his anger against sin was more than satisfied. Are you living in fear of God's condemnation or in the freedom of his grace? Explain.

11. For generations Israel wanted God's protection and provision but withheld their devotion and obedience. They prayed for God's justice against their enemies, but never imagined God's justice would result in their judgment. Does that sound at all like the church today? Why or why not?

12. What should the church's response be to that reality?

Praise God for his abundant grace and mercy. Then ask him to help you to never take his grace for granted or to misuse grace as a cover for sinfulness.

NOW OR LATER

In Leviticus 26, the Lord explained to Israel the rewards for obedience to his commands and the consequences for disobedience. Read Leviticus 26:14-39. How many of these punishments are repeated in Ezekiel 5?

What remedy does God offer to Israel in Leviticus 26:40-45 if they failed to obey his commands?

How might the people in exile in Ezekiel's day have applied those truths to their situation?

FOUR

GOD'S GLORY DEPARTS

Ezekiel 8:1-18; 10:3-5, 18-19; 11:17-24

My **older brother** and I had a rocky childhood relationship. We would argue and shout and occasionally come to blows. The arguments and fighting would instantly stop, however, if our mom or dad walked through the door. To them it looked like all was peaceful on the home front, but the reality was far different.

Group Discussion. Recount a time you were caught by a parent (or teacher or employer) doing something you shouldn't have been doing. What were the consequences?

Personal Reflection. Do you ever act as if God can't see you or wonder why God doesn't punish someone who seems to behave badly and never gets caught? How do you explain those situations?

Ezekiel 8–11 are one extended vision from the Lord. Ezekiel has been in exile six years. The group of Israelites in exile with him thought God would never allow Jerusalem to fall to outside invasion. They based this belief on the fact that God's temple stood in Jerusalem and God's visible glory dwelled in the temple's innermost sanctuary, resting over the ark of the covenant.

The Israelites still living in Jerusalem, however, were acting like the Lord had already abandoned them. They had an outward appearance of religious piety but had brought in pagan elements from the nations around them. God will expose the reality of Israel's disobedience, and

Ezekiel will watch as the glory of God's presence leaves the temple. The people in Jerusalem didn't see it; Ezekiel had the eyes of God to see what was really happening. The temple had become an empty box spiritually. Four walls and a roof, expensive furniture and ornaments remain, but there is no longer the abiding presence of the Lord. *Read Ezekiel 8:1-18.*

1. Ezekiel is shown exactly how the people of God have forsaken their covenant promises to the Lord. Make a list of the "utterly detestable things" (v. 6) God reveals to Ezekiel.

2. Think about your relationship to God and your worship of him. How might some of these same "detestable things" creep into our lives and what would they look like?

3. How does God respond to these sins in the temple (vv. 6, 18)?

4. How might God respond to such hidden and secret acts of sin and disobedience in our lives?

5. The priests of Israel seemed to be going through the outward motions of worshiping the Lord (v. 11), but "in the darkness" they were insulting God by their actions. How could that be the situation today in the church?

6. What would you say to someone who says, "God doesn't really see me or care about what I do in my personal life"?

7. *Read Ezekiel 10:3-5, 18-19.* Ezekiel again sees the chariot throne of God he first saw in chapter one. Trace the departure of the glory of the Lord from the inner room of the temple to the chariot throne of the Lord (vv. 4, 18-19).

8. In our age, God's presence inhabits the gathered believers. We together become God's temple (1 Corinthians 3:16). What do you look for in your church gathering or small group as the evidence of God's presence?

9. Ezekiel sees the glorious presence of the Lord depart from the temple, but the people in Jerusalem seem unaware of what was happening. If God's presence would leave your church gathering, do you think you would notice it? Explain.

10. *Read Ezekiel 11:17-24.* Is your devotion to the Lord undivided, or are you still drawn and pulled toward your old life before you began to follow Jesus?

11. What does God suggest as a corrective measure to a divided heart (11:18-20)?

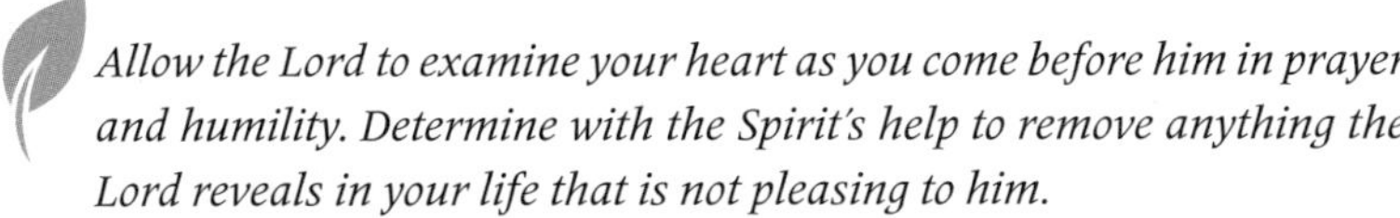

Allow the Lord to examine your heart as you come before him in prayer and humility. Determine with the Spirit's help to remove anything the Lord reveals in your life that is not pleasing to him.

NOW OR LATER

At the end of our study, the glory of the Lord left Jerusalem and stopped "above the mountain east of it" (Ezekiel 11:23). When the prophet Zechariah many years later talks about the Lord coming in majesty to deliver his people, he says, "On that day his feet will stand on the Mount of Olives, east of Jerusalem" (Zechariah 14:4). Many Bible teachers believe that when Jesus returns in glory, he will come back to the very place where the glory of God departed from Israel in Ezekiel's day.

To learn more about when the glory of God's presence first filled the tabernacle and later the temple, read Exodus 40:33-38 and 1 Kings 8:10-11.

FIVE

TRAMPLING THE GRACE OF GOD

Ezekiel 16:1-34, 59-63

Rebecca Pippert tells a powerful story about a friend whose wife came to him and said, "I haven't loved you for a long time, and I want a divorce." The husband was crushed by his wife's rejection and began to pray for her and love her more deeply than ever before. Friends and Christian leaders told him to find someone new and move on, but God's response was clear: "Would you really do to her what I would never do to you?"

The husband continued to pray and fast—for nine years! In time, the marriage was restored. The faithful lover summed up the entire experience like this: "Nothing is ever lost in the kingdom of God; not one tear or prayer is wasted."

Group Discussion. What would you have advised this husband to do? How could you have supported his pursuit to restore the marriage?

Personal Reflection. Have you ever felt unwanted and rejected? How about deeply loved and valued? Which do you sense most often from God?

Ezekiel 16 contains some of the most graphic language in Scripture. If it were sold as a music download, a warning label for explicit content would be attached. The people of Israel had rejected the Lord to prostitute themselves with other gods. Sin isn't polite, and Ezekiel sees no reason to be polite about it. But as shocking as the actions of God's people are, it is God's love that takes our breath away. In a world filled with abandonment and unfaithfulness, God demonstrates his remarkable, astonishing love. *Read Ezekiel 16:1-34.*

1. Based on Ezekiel's description of an unwanted child (vv. 1-3), how would you describe Israel's origins and beginning?

2. What was God's response to this abandoned child (vv. 6-7)?

3. How does Jerusalem's status parallel our spiritual condition, and what God did to rescue us?

4. When Israel became an adult, God took her as his wife and entered into a covenant of marriage with her (v. 8). What spiritual and material blessings did he lavish on her (vv. 8-14)?

5. Instead of valuing those gifts, Israel treated them with contempt. What are the spiritual realities behind the description of Israel's unfaithfulness in verses 15-19?

6. Why is it significant that the people of Israel "did not remember the days of [their] youth" (v. 22)?

7. What happens in us if we do not remember our past condition and God's grace in saving us?

8. How does Israel's spiritual prostitution exceed what we normally consider adultery and unfaithfulness (vv. 30-34)?

9. Do you think of your sin as adultery and unfaithfulness to the Lord? Or do you just think you have broken the rules? Explain.

10. *Read Ezekiel 16:59-63.* If Israel were our wife, most of us would dissolve the marriage based on repeated adultery and irreconcilable differences, but God moves in a different direction. What does he promise to do (vv. 62-63)?

11. How does God's love and forgiveness offered to you make you feel about yourself?

12. Based on this passage, how would you explain God's love to a person who doesn't know him?

Think back to the path of sin and death you were on before Jesus saved you. Consider God's willingness to lay all that you deserved (bad consequences, wrath, and judgment) on Jesus. Thank God for his relentless love.

NOW OR LATER

Do you think God would use any of the language of Ezekiel 16 to refer to our nation or the church today? Why or why not?

What would he say about how we have used his gifts to us?

Write a few "verses" of the Lord's admonition to us. Include the provisions of his grace as well.

SIX

THE LORD SEARCHES

Ezekiel 22:1-31

When I was a boy, the worst words I could hear from my mother were, "Just wait until your father comes home." The waiting alone was dreadful, but I knew discipline was coming. I would have to stand in front of my dad and confess what I had done, and it had to be the full truth or Dad would consult with Mom to fill out any details I had missed. Then the sentence of discipline was passed and there was no escape.

Group Discussion. Tell the group about a memorable childhood discipline from a parent or teacher. Did you ever try to escape punishment by hiding or blaming someone else?

Personal Reflection. When you do something wrong, do you tend to ignore it or dismiss it? Or do you worry over the punishment that might come? What is the biblical remedy when we do wrong?

The people living in Jerusalem were supposed to bring the light of God's holiness and grace to the world. But in Ezekiel's day they were living just like the world around them. Their sins were long-standing, and their hearts were unrepentant. God's judgment was about to fall, but judgment could be turned away if just one person would stand for God. *Read Ezekiel 22:1-22.*

1. As you review this passage, what are the sins God names against his people?

2. Are there sins on God's list that don't seem to rise to the same level as murder or bloodshed?

3. Who are injured or harmed by the action of the people (vv. 6-11), and why does God point them out?

4. Which of the sins in this chapter might we as God's people be involved in but convince ourselves that God does not see or will not punish us?

5. God asks a question in verse 14 to force Israel to think about their sin and how they will answer God in the day of judgment. Ask yourself the same question. What will you cling to in the face of God's judgment: your best efforts or God's grace? Explain.

6. The Lord pictures Israel as metals placed in a furnace (vv. 17-22). What is the dross God wants to purify from them?

7. How does God purify us as his children?

8. What is the result in our lives of passing through the furnace of God's discipline?

9. *Read Ezekiel 22:23-31.* What groups does God call out in this passage, and what has each group done or failed to do toward God's people?

What groups would God call out in our society, and what sins might he lay at their feet?

10. God searches for one person to stand in the gap for his people (vv. 30-31). What is God searching for in that person?

11. What are the results of God's search and what happens because of it?

12. Do you qualify as the person to hold off God's judgment in our culture? Explain your response.

Are you courageous enough to pray that you would be the person to stand in the gap for God's people? If you are, ask God to begin to develop the qualities in your life that will make you adequate for that task. If you are not willing to be that person, ask God to change your heart.

NOW OR LATER

Read through the Ten Commandments in Exodus 20:1-17. Now look again at the sins of Jerusalem in Ezekiel 22:1-22. How many of God's basic laws were being broken?

SEVEN

COUNTING THE COST

Ezekiel 24:15-27

Russell and Darlene Deibler arrived in New Guinea on their first wedding anniversary. They had come to share the message of Christ, but when the Japanese army invaded the island, the two were separated. Russell was sent to a concentration camp and soon died.

Darlene was imprisoned in a separate camp where she suffered years of forced labor, indignity, sickness, and near starvation. One day she was singled out for execution and locked in a small death cell. As the door slammed behind her, Darlene fell to her knees in a cold sweat of terror only to find herself singing a song she had learned in Sunday school.

Fear not, little flock, whatever your lot,
He enters all rooms, "the doors being shut."*

Darlene felt strong arms around her. She knew that though her captors could lock her in, they could not lock out her Lord. She knew that God would never put her where his presence could not sustain her. That assurance carried her through impossible times and preserved her life until liberation came.**

Group Discussion. Under what circumstances have you most clearly sensed God's presence and comfort?

Personal Reflection. When have you felt yourself to be far from the Lord? How was that sense of closeness with him restored?

---

*Paul Rader, "Fear Not, Little Flock," 1921.

**Darlene Deibler Rose, *Evidence Not Seen* (New York: HarperCollins, 1988).

Ezekiel's acceptance of God's call to be a prophet was the big yes in Ezekiel's life. He was willing to be fully God's and to bear whatever burden came his way. But the big yes was followed by a lifetime of smaller yeses as each new directive came from the Lord. *Read Ezekiel 24:15-27.*

1. What questions about God's goodness and love does this passage raise?

2. How do you feel toward Ezekiel: sorrowful, angry that he doesn't argue with God, upset because he just went along?

3. Is it possible to put conditions on our allegiance to the Lord—to trust him and follow him only when our lives are comfortable? Explain.

4. In what ways are you challenged by Ezekiel's faithfulness and sacrifice?

5. God not only takes Ezekiel's wife, but he also won't allow Ezekiel to mourn publicly. This was to show the people in captivity that when the city of Jerusalem fell to the Babylonian army and their relatives were killed, they, being seven hundred miles away, wouldn't even know about it. They will just continue to live as they normally do. Is Ezekiel's wife just an object for God to use to prove a point to the people? How would you justify God's action?

6. How does God show grace to Ezekiel?

7. Have you experienced unexpected loss or pain? How did you respond to it?

8. If God asked you to go through Ezekiel's experience just so the people around you would get a message about coming judgment in their lives, would you (1) trust God and obey him, (2) argue with God about fairness, (3) or question whether it was really the Lord speaking to you? Explain.

9. The captives would not hear about Jerusalem's fall from a news report but from a survivor who would stumble into Babylon weeks later (vv. 25-27). How will that fugitive's report help to convince the people in captivity that God is the sovereign Lord (vv. 24, 27)?

10. Israel as the bride or wife of the Lord had separated herself from him by following other gods. In what other context did God experience separation from or the death of a loved one?

11. What is the delight of your eyes (see v. 25)? What would hurt most if God took it from you?

12. What does it mean to surrender all your life to God?

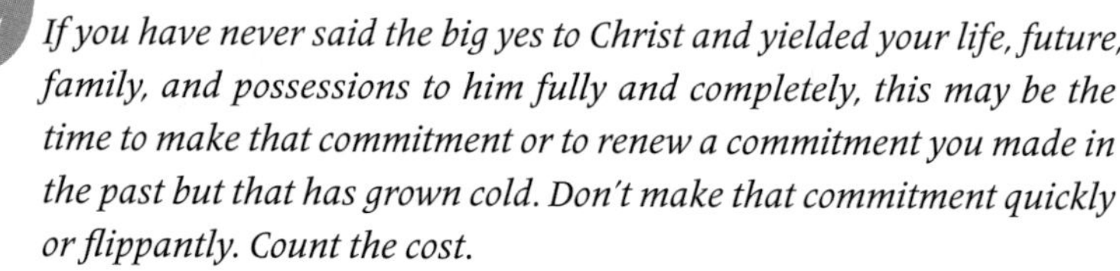
If you have never said the big yes to Christ and yielded your life, future, family, and possessions to him fully and completely, this may be the time to make that commitment or to renew a commitment you made in the past but that has grown cold. Don't make that commitment quickly or flippantly. Count the cost.

NOW OR LATER

Romans 12:1-2 is the New Testament call to wholehearted commitment to Jesus. In a decisive act of our will, we give ourselves to him as a living sacrifice. Then, as we move through life, we continue to surrender, to say yes to whatever he asks us to do. Read Romans 12:1-2 carefully. Explain Ezekiel's obedience in the words of that passage.

EIGHT

RECEIVING A NEW HEART

Ezekiel 36:16-38

My **eighty-something** Aunt Virginia is a courageous witness for Jesus to her family and her community. When her nephew was diagnosed with cancer, she came right to the point with him about eternity. As she faithfully shared the message and as the Spirit of God worked in his heart, her nephew put his trust in Jesus as Savior and Lord, and he was made a new creature.

The transformation in that man's life was dramatic. His old habits were left behind. He began to tell others how Jesus had cleansed his life and made him a new man. The cancer eventually took his physical life, but he is alive forever in Christ.

Group Discussion. Do you have, or have you heard, a dramatic conversion story? Tell it to the group. Does it take more grace to transform a notorious sinner than for a typical sinner?

Personal Reflection. Would someone observing your life, hearing your words, and watching your spending habits conclude that you are a follower of Jesus? What would convince them?

Ezekiel grieved over the people of Israel just as many Christians grieve over our own nation. We see God's character insulted and mocked, and we wonder if God's judgment will fall on us. As Ezekiel contemplated his people's sinfulness, God came to him one day with an astonishing promise of grace and cleansing. *Read Ezekiel 36:16-38.*

1. How had Israel sinned against God and profaned his name and character (vv. 16-22)?

2. Would you say our culture and nation is guilty of some of the same things God's people were guilty of? What specifically are we guilty of?

3. What do verses 22-23 tell you about the actions of God toward Israel and why he does what he does?

4. What do verses 22-23 say about the things God does or doesn't do in your life?

5. God makes some incredible promises in this chapter, and they have been interpreted and applied in two different ways. First, these verses are spoken to Israel. (See question eleven for the second way.) What does God say he will do for Israel in verses 22-30?

6. Does Israel deserve what God will give them? Why or why not?

7. If God cleanses Israel, why will they remember their evil ways and wicked deeds (vv. 31-32)?

8. Does God ever want us to feel guilt or shame about our sin even after he forgives us? Explain.

9. Do you think God has already kept all these promises to Israel (vv. 33-38), or are some yet to be fulfilled—or has God failed in some of his promises? Explain.

10. Does Israel have any part to play in their own restoration (v. 37)?

11. Another way to apply this chapter is to see it as a foreshadowing of how God will work in people's hearts under the new covenant sealed by the death and resurrection of Jesus. Through faith in him, we are cleansed and made new. Receiving a new heart and new spirit (vv. 26-27) refer to being made a new creation in Christ by the presence of God's Holy Spirit. From this same perspective, how would you explain prospering in the land (vv. 28-30)?

12. When we ask for forgiveness should we focus on our sinfulness or on God holiness? What difference would this make?

13. Who could you engage in a spiritual conversation with this week? What would you want to tell this person about Ezekiel 36 and God's promises?

Give God praise for the work of cleansing and restoration he has done in your life. Ask God to give you the courage to take the opportunity to share his message of transformation with someone else.

NOW OR LATER

Christians often talk about salvation as "Jesus coming into our hearts." Is that an accurate way to describe salvation? How would you say it differently using the language of Ezekiel 36?

NINE

CAN THESE BONES LIVE?

Ezekiel 37:1-14

Just before Thanksgiving, teams from our church delivered food in one of the poorest sections of our city. At the end of one subdivision was an abandoned mobile home park. The homes were collapsing or had been stripped of their aluminum siding. Our team decided to drive through anyway, and in the back of the park we found families living in previously abandoned homes. As we took groceries to the door, gaunt little children came to stand by their mothers. It looked like a scene out of a destitute, majority-world country. One little guy's face floated in my head (and heart) after our encounter. I drove back a couple of weeks later, but the family was gone. I prayed and cried for that family and for that young boy. Their situation seemed so hopeless.

Group Discussion. Describe a scene or situation you have witnessed that seemed beyond repair or hope. What did you ask God to do? What did you do?

Personal Reflection. What circumstance or relationship in your life is most in need of God's reviving power right now? What do you want God to do? What can you do?

God asked the prophet Ezekiel to do some pretty strange things: shave off his hair, burn some of it, and eat a scroll. But probably the strangest thing God ever asked Ezekiel to do is in this chapter. He asked

Ezekiel to preach to a bunch of dried up, long-dead human bones—and Ezekiel obeyed! *Read Ezekiel 37:1-14.*

1. Do you think this was a literal valley of bones, or did Ezekiel see this in another realm? What statements in verse 1 bring you to your conclusion?

2. What was the purpose behind God asking Ezekiel to walk back and forth among the bones (v. 3)?

3. In verse 11 God tells Ezekiel what the bones represent. What does the prophet's vision convey to you about the spiritual condition of Israel before God?

4. What does God declare his intention to be with the bones (vv. 5-6)?

5. What does your answer to question four mean when applied to the people of Israel?

6. What correlation do you see between what God intended to do in Israel and what God set out to do in your heart and life?

7. What was Ezekiel's part in the accomplishment of God's purpose (vv. 4, 9)?

8. What would you have found difficult about obeying God's command to Ezekiel to prophesy?

9. Describe the two stages in the revival of the bones (vv. 8-10).

10. Right now, in which of the two stages is your church or family or Bible study group? Explain.

11. The words *breath*, *wind*, and *Spirit* are all the same Hebrew word. What is God's role in bringing new life to dead situations or hopeless people?

12. What similarities do you see between what happened in the valley of dry bones and what Jesus might do in a hopeless situation or in a dead relationship in your life?

13. What steps of obedience do you need to take?

Commit any dead or hopeless situations in your life to the Spirit. Ask him to blow his life-giving breath over you.

NOW OR LATER

If you could speak to the dry bones of the church today, what would you say? Is there anyone speaking this message to the church right now? What can you do to support that person and help spread the message?

TEN

WORSHIP IN GOD'S NEW TEMPLE

Ezekiel 43:1-12

Tucked away in the streets of downtown Chicago is the Holy Name Cathedral Church. When I walk into that place, my eyes and heart are drawn upward by the towering pillars and arches that seem to disappear into the heavens. I am struck silent by the visual reminder of the majesty and glory of God. I find myself worshiping God, who dwells far above us.

During a trip to Uganda a few years ago, I joined a congregation for worship in what I could only describe as a toolshed. Its gravel floor and corrugated metal sides and roof reminded me that Jesus became poor for us. I was struck by the joy-filled faces and exuberant singing of the people of God gathered in Jesus' name. I found myself worshiping God who came down as far as sin had taken us to set us free and to give us life.

Group Discussion. Describe a memorable place where you were drawn into worship of God. What did that place convey to you about God?

Personal Reflection. Where do you feel closest to God? What is it about that place that stirs your heart to worship?

In Ezekiel's final vision (Ezekiel 40–48), he sees God's temple in Jerusalem restored. Students of the book disagree on when this temple was or will be built. Some think it was an idealized version of the temple built when the people of Israel returned from captivity in Babylon. Others believe it is a symbolic representation of the church, the temple of the Holy Spirit in this present age. Still others contend that this temple will be built during Christ's future kingdom.

We may have differing views on *when* this temple will be built, but the *purpose* of the temple is clear. God's people are invited to worship the Lord with joy and gladness. The glory of the Lord that left the temple because of Israel's rebellion will now return to dwell among a restored people.

At the beginning of the vision in chapter 40, Ezekiel encounters a man (v. 3) who acts as his guide through the temple. He leads the prophet to the gate of the temple that faces east. *Read Ezekiel 43:1-12.*

1. As you read this passage, do you get the impression that God was giving his people more than just a construction plan to follow? What was God demonstrating about himself?

2. Earlier Ezekiel saw the glorious presence of the Lord depart from the temple in Jerusalem (see study four). Now the prophet sees God's glory return. Contrast the spiritual condition of the worshipers when the glory departed with the spiritual condition of the worshipers when the glory returns (vv. 7, 9).

3. How did Ezekiel respond to his vision of the glory of the Lord (vv. 2-5)?

4. How do you experience the glory of the Lord?

5. How would God's declaration of his intention to live among his people forever (v. 7) affect the Israelites already in captivity?

6. In what ways does God dwell with Christians, we who live under the new covenant?

7. The whole area of this restored temple will be considered "most holy" (v. 12)—set apart for God's purpose, uncontaminated by sin, pure. In this present age, God resides in bodies, not buildings. The apostle Paul in 1 Corinthians 6:19 says, "Your bodies are temples of the Holy Spirit, who is in you." How should that truth affect how we live, the places we go, what we put into our bodies, and how we view and care for our physical bodies?

8. God's temple today is also the gathered body of believers. In 1 Corinthians 3:16, Paul writes: "Don't you know that you yourselves [plural, referring to the gathered group of Christians] are God's temple and that God's Spirit dwells in your midst?" When you walk into a worship service, you are entering God's holy temple, not the building but the visible body of Christ. How does that affect your attitude and focus during worship?

9. Ezekiel focused his message on judgment and restoration, our failure and God's grace. Which aspect of his message has spoken most directly to your life and why?

10. How have you responded to God's message?

11. Would you have wanted to be Ezekiel? What do you think would have been the hardest part of his ministry and what would have brought the most blessing?

Pray that God's message to you through Ezekiel would continue to produce fruit in your life and that you will respond obediently to God's call.

NOW OR LATER

We only read and examined selected passages in Ezekiel in this study guide. Make a plan to read the whole book, whether in two or three larger sections, a chapter a day, or a paragraph a day. Keep a journal, and ask what God is calling you to do in response to what you read. Then do it! If there is a friend who will read the book with you, talk about each passage and hold each other accountable to read and to obey.

LEADER'S NOTES

My grace is sufficient for you.

2 CORINTHIANS 12:9

Leading a Bible discussion can be an enjoyable and rewarding experience. But it can also be scary—especially if you've never done it before. If this is your feeling, you're in good company. When God asked Moses to lead the Israelites out of Egypt, he replied, "Please send someone else" (Exodus 4:13)! It was the same with Solomon, Jeremiah, and Timothy, but God helped these people in spite of their weaknesses, and he will help you as well.

You don't need to be an expert on the Bible or a trained teacher to lead a Bible discussion. The idea behind these inductive studies is that the leader guides group members to discover for themselves what the Bible has to say. This method of learning will allow group members to remember much more of what is said than a lecture would.

These studies are designed to be led easily. As a matter of fact, the flow of questions through the passage from observation to interpretation to application is so natural that you may feel that the studies lead themselves. This study guide is also flexible. You can use it with a variety of groups—student, professional, neighborhood, or church groups. Each study takes forty-five to sixty minutes in a group setting.

There are some important facts to know about group dynamics and encouraging discussion. The suggestions listed below should enable you to effectively and enjoyably fulfill your role as leader.

PREPARING FOR THE STUDY

1. Ask God to help you understand and apply the passage in your own life. Unless this happens, you will not be prepared to lead others. Pray too for the various members of the group. Ask God to open your hearts to the message of his Word and motivate you to action.

2. Read the introduction to the guide to get an overview of the entire book and the issues that will be explored.

3. As you begin each study, read and re-read the assigned Bible passage to familiarize yourself with it.

4. This study guide is based on the New International Version of the Bible. It will help you and the group if you use this translation as the basis for your study and discussion.

5. Carefully work through each question in the study. Spend time in meditation and reflection as you consider how to respond.

6. Write your thoughts and responses in the space provided in the study guide. This will help you to express your understanding of the passage clearly.

7. It might help to have a Bible dictionary handy. Use it to look up any unfamiliar words, names, or places. (For additional help on how to study a passage, see chapter five of *How to Lead a LifeGuide Bible Study*, InterVarsity Press.)

8. Consider how you can apply the Scripture to your life. Remember that the group will follow your lead in responding to the studies. They will not go any deeper than you do.

9. Once you have finished your own study of the passage, familiarize yourself with the leader's notes for the study you are leading. These are designed to help you in several ways. First, they tell you the purpose the study guide author had in mind when writing the study. Take time to think through how the study questions work together to accomplish that purpose. Second, the notes provide you with additional background information or suggestions on group dynamics for various questions. This information can be useful when people have difficulty understanding or answering a question. Third, the leader's notes can alert you to potential problems you may encounter during the study.

10. If you wish to remind yourself of anything mentioned in the leader's notes, make a note to yourself below that question in the study.

LEADING THE STUDY

1. Begin the study on time. Open with prayer, asking God to help the group to understand and apply the passage.

2. Be sure that everyone in your group has a study guide. Encourage the group to prepare beforehand for each discussion by reading the introduction to the guide and by working through the questions in the study.

3. At the beginning of your first time together, explain that these studies are meant to be discussions, not lectures. Encourage the members of the group to participate. However, do not put pressure on those who may be hesitant to speak during the first few sessions. You may want to suggest the following guidelines to your group.

- Stick to the topic being discussed.
- Your responses should be based on the verses that are the focus of the discussion and not on outside authorities such as commentaries or speakers.
- These studies focus on a particular passage of Scripture. Only rarely should you refer to other portions of the Bible. This allows for everyone to participate in in-depth study on equal ground.
- Anything said in the group is considered confidential and will not be discussed outside the group unless specific permission is given to do so.
- We will listen attentively to each other and provide time for each person present to talk.
- We will pray for each other.

4. Have a group member read the introduction at the beginning of the discussion.

5. Every session begins with a group discussion question. The question or activity is meant to be used before the passage is read. The question introduces the theme of the study and encourages group members to begin to open up. Encourage as many members as possible to participate, and be ready to get the discussion going with your own response.

This section is designed to reveal where our thoughts or feelings need to be transformed by Scripture. That is why it is especially important not to read the passage before the discussion question is asked. The passage will tend to color the honest reactions people would otherwise give because they are, of course, supposed to think the way the Bible does.

You may want to supplement the group discussion question with an icebreaker to help people get comfortable. See the community section of *Small Group Idea Book* for more ideas.

You also might want to use the personal reflection question with your group. Either allow a time of silence for people to respond individually or discuss it together.

6. Have a group member (or members if the passage is long) read aloud the passage to be studied. Then give people several minutes to read the passage again silently so that they can take it all in.

7. Question 1 will generally be an overview question designed to briefly survey the passage. Encourage the group to look at the whole passage, but try to avoid getting sidetracked by questions or issues that will be addressed later in the study.

8. As you ask the questions, keep in mind that they are designed to be used just as they are written. You may simply read them aloud. Or you may prefer to express them in your own words.

There may be times when it is appropriate to deviate from the study guide. For example, a question may have already been answered. If so, move on to the next question. Or someone may raise an important question not covered in the guide. Take time to discuss it, but try to keep the group from going off on tangents.

9. Avoid answering your own questions. If necessary, repeat or rephrase them until they are clearly understood. Or point out something you read in the leader's notes to clarify the context or meaning. An eager group quickly becomes passive and silent if they think the leader will do most of the talking.

10. Don't be afraid of silence. People may need time to think about the question before formulating their answers.

11. Don't be content with just one answer. Ask, "What do the rest of you think?" or "Anything else?" until several people have given answers to the question.

12. Acknowledge all contributions. Try to be affirming whenever possible. Never reject an answer. If it is clearly off base, ask, "Which verse led you to that conclusion?" or again, "What do the rest of you think?"

13. Don't expect every answer to be addressed to you, even though this will probably happen at first. As group members become more at ease, they will begin to truly interact with each other. This is one sign of healthy discussion.

14. Don't be afraid of controversy. It can be very stimulating. If you don't resolve an issue completely, don't be frustrated. Move on and keep it in mind for later. A subsequent study may solve the problem.

15. Periodically summarize what the group has said about the passage. This helps to draw together the various ideas mentioned and gives continuity to the study. But don't preach.

16. At the end of the Bible discussion you may want to allow group members a time of quiet to work on an idea under "Now or Later." Then discuss what you experienced. Or you may want to encourage group members to work on these ideas between meetings. Give an opportunity during the session for people to talk about what they are learning.

17. Conclude your time together with conversational prayer, adapting the prayer suggestion at the end of the study to your group. Ask for God's help in following through on the commitments you've made.

18. End on time.

Many more suggestions and helps are found in *How to Lead a LifeGuide Bible Study*.

COMPONENTS OF SMALL GROUPS

A healthy small group should do more than study the Bible. There are four components to consider as you structure your time together.

Nurture. Small groups help us to grow in our knowledge and love of God. Bible study is the key to making this happen and is the foundation of your small group.

Community. Small groups are a great place to develop deep friendships with other Christians. Allow time for informal interaction before and after each study. Plan activities and games that will help you get to know each other. Spend time having fun together going on a picnic or cooking dinner together.

Worship and prayer. Your study will be enhanced by spending time praising God together in prayer or song. Pray for each other's needs and keep track of how God is answering prayer in your group. Ask God to help you to apply what you are learning in your study.

Outreach. Reaching out to others can be a practical way of applying what you are learning, and it will keep your group from becoming self-focused. Host a series of evangelistic discussions for your friends or neighbors. Clean up the yard of an elderly friend. Serve at a soup kitchen together, or spend a day working on a Habitat house.

Many more suggestions and helps in each of these areas are found in Small Group Idea Book. Information on building a small group can be found in *Small Group Leaders' Handbook* and *The Big Book on Small Groups* (both from InterVarsity Press). Reading through one of these books would be worth your time.

Before each study, you may want to put an asterisk by the key questions you think are most important for your group to cover, in case you don't have time to cover all the questions. As we suggested in "Getting the Most Out of *Ezekiel*," if you want to make sure you have enough time to discuss all the questions, you have other options. For example, the group could decide to extend each meeting to ninety minutes or more. Alternatively, you could devote two sixty-minute sessions to each study.

STUDY 1. APPROACHING THE GOD OF GLORY. EZEKIEL 1:1-28

PURPOSE: To be impressed with God's powerful and majestic presence and to respond to him appropriately in worship.

Introduction. Ezekiel 1-3 present us with the prophet's inaugural vision and his call to be God's spokesperson to the exiles in Babylon. While the people were captives in Babylon, they were not slaves. Thus, they were not required to work for the Babylonians. The people of Judah were allowed to build homes and live in peace. They were not permitted to return to Jerusalem, but they were free to worship God and live in their own community.

Question 1. You might want to use a white board to draw or sketch the various components of the vision. Don't get too bogged down in drawing all the details but try to envision the immensity and power of what Ezekiel saw and heard.

Question 3. God does not usually wait for people to find their way to him. Instead, he is a seeking God who comes to us where we are and speaks to our situation as it is, not as we wish it to be. The exiles must have felt far from God, but God was already in their place of exile, waiting to speak to them. Apply that truth to your group. God is present wherever you are on your spiritual journey. "For Ezekiel, the experience of God's presence came in a foreign place, Babylon. But more than that, it was a place in which neither he nor his companions expected the divine presence. . . . There is no place and no circumstances in which the experience of God may be denied" (Peter Craigie, *Ezekiel*, Daily Study Bible [Louisville, KY: Westminster John Knox, 1983], 13).

Question 4. The four living creatures are later identified as cherubim or cherubs (Ezekiel 10:1-5, 15, 20), powerful angelic beings who are associated with the protection of God's glory. The apostle John sees them around God's throne in Revelation 4–5. Cherubs guard God's holy presence and carry out his judgment. After Adam and Eve were expelled from the Garden of Eden, cherubs guarded the way back to the tree of life (Genesis 3:23-24). Cherubs were depicted in the tabernacle and later in the temple in Jerusalem (Exodus 25:18-22; 26:1; 1 Kings 6:22-35).

Question 5. The structure of the wheels is difficult to envision, but it probably looked like a gyroscope. Topaz is a crystal-like mineral and is light green to gold in color. The eyes may be gleams of light from the facets of the topaz or literal eyes depicting God's all-knowing nature. The ability to move in any direction instantly without turning is a depiction of God's all-present nature.

Questions 6 and 7. Ezekiel hears the vibration of the wings of the four living creatures, a sound like an army on the move or the roar of a massive waterfall. He also hears a voice, likely God's voice (v. 25). God can speak to us in a voice or a vision. More often God speaks through his written Word, through the inner prompting of his Holy Spirit or even through the counsel of godly believers.

Question 9. Terror and falling down are common responses to being in the presence of a holy God (see Isaiah 6:1-5; Revelation 1:10-18). Falling down reveals our humility and awe before the glorious God of the universe.

Question 10. God's revelation of himself to Ezekiel was obviously designed to show the prophet what kind of God he was being called to serve. Try to discover what aspect of God's character most impressed each of the group members.

STUDY 2. THE PREPARATION OF A PROPHET. EZEKIEL 2:1–3:15

PURPOSE: To bring us to the place where we will listen to God's call in our lives and will respond with obedience and willingness.

Question 1. Ezekiel spoke to the people of Judah who were in exile in Babylon. Five years of exile had not brought them to repentance. They "have been in revolt against me *to this very day*" (Ezekiel 2:3; emphasis added). God calls them "obstinate and stubborn" (Ezekiel 2:4), "rebellious" (Ezekiel 2:3, 5, 6), and compares them to "briers," "thorns," and "scorpions" (Ezekiel 2:6).

Question 2. The characterization of the people of Israel as rebels is a distinctive theme of Ezekiel. This has been a deep-seated, generational sin among God's people ("they and their ancestors have been in revolt against me" [v. 3]). Ezekiel, in contrast, is not to be rebellious (v. 8) but obedient to God's word.

Question 3. A person's audience is anyone God has placed in their life who needs to hear the gospel or needs encouragement in their walk with the Lord: coworkers, believing or unbelieving family members, and friends. Even if we have spoken to them in the past and have been rejected, God calls us to continue to look and pray for opportunities to speak God's truth.

Question 5. God's command to eat the scroll was an immediate test of Ezekiel's obedience. Would he obey, or would he be like the rebellious people around him? The scroll represented God's message Ezekiel was to speak to the people. He did not speak a message he had composed but one he received from God. Furthermore, there was no room for any additions or alterations by Ezekiel. The scroll was filled front and back.

Question 6. Ezekiel is to listen to God's words and then to absorb them into his heart and mind like food is absorbed into the body. Because no one among the people would listen to God's message and all would stand in opposition to him, Ezekiel may have assumed that the scroll would taste bitter. But obedience to God, even in difficult circumstances, always brings a sense of joy and satisfaction.

Question 7. We absorb God's truth by listening carefully and responding willingly to whatever God says to us in his word. Colossians 3:16 says: "Let the message of Christ dwell among you richly as you teach and admonish one another with all wisdom."

Question 9. How often have we listened to God's Word and even sensed God's Spirit prompting us to a new level of obedience and then walked away unchanged? The temptation to those who teach God's message is to change or water down the message to make it more palatable to contemporary culture.

Question 10. God promised Ezekiel that the message would be God's message, not a message the prophet would have to compose or defend. God also promised the presence of his strengthening Spirit in the prophet's life (Ezekiel 2:2). The Holy Spirit was present and active in the Old Testament, especially to empower God's prophets and to oversee the faithful writing and preservation of their words. Finally, God promised courage for the prophet. The people may be hardened and resistant, but Ezekiel would be even more determined in his proclamation (Ezekiel 3:8-9).

Question 12. Many Christians are content with knowledge of God's truth but have never grasped it and absorbed it as their own. Many more of us know God's Word and believe it, but we have yet to sense any burden to tell anyone else about it.

STUDY 3. WITNESSING GOD'S JUDGMENT. EZEKIEL 5:1-17

PURPOSE: To help us think seriously about God's judgment—and God's grace.

Questions 1. Shaving the head and the beard were signs of mourning (Isaiah 15:2; Jeremiah 48:37) and disgrace (2 Samuel 10:4-5). Priests were not to trim their beards even in times of great sorrow (Leviticus 21:5). The coming destruction of Jerusalem would make even the most intense personal tragedy seem small.

Question 2. The hairs represent the people still in Jerusalem, and the disposal of the three piles of hair indicates the fate of the city's citizens.

Question 3. The symbolism is clear. A third of the inhabitants would be destroyed within the city, a third would be killed by the sword in fighting, and a third would be scattered among the nations and harassed by hostile forces. Only a handful of people would survive—a few hairs concealed in Ezekiel's robe. This surviving remnant would be the evidence of God's grace. All deserved to perish, but a few would be saved.

Question 5. The phrase, "This is Jerusalem" (v. 5), points back to Ezekiel 4:1, where Ezekiel is told by God to take a tile (or brick) and engrave a sketch of Jerusalem on it. The failure of the people of Jerusalem was that despite all of God's blessings, they had rebelled against him and his laws. Even worse, the people had exceeded the other nations in wickedness. "Unparalleled sin demands unparalleled judgment" (John Taylor, *Ezekiel*, Tyndale Old Testament Commentaries [Downers Grove, IL: InterVarsity Press, 1969], 86). Babylon was certainly set against Jerusalem, but now an even greater adversary arises: "This is what the Sovereign LORD says: 'I myself am against you, Jerusalem'" (v. 8).

Questions 6 and 7. There were undoubtedly some faithful, godly Israelites in Jerusalem, one being the prophet Jeremiah. It is not unusual for a godly remnant to be swept up in the backwash of God's judgment on a larger population. God may have seen fit to rescue those who were godly as well.

Question 8. God's wrath against sin was fully satisfied by Jesus' willing sacrifice on the cross. God now freely forgives those who come to him in faith. God may discipline a Christian, but we will not face consuming judgment or condemnation. God's wrath will be poured out, however, on those who reject his gracious offer of forgiveness (Romans 1:18; Revelation 6:15-17).

Question 11. This question is not designed to prompt attacks on the church but to promote a serious discussion about how the church (like Israel) might take God's grace and favor for granted and even use his abundant grace to hide or permit the most grievous sins.

STUDY 4. GOD'S GLORY DEPARTS. EZEKIEL 8:1-18; 10:3-5, 18-19; 11:17-24

PURPOSE: To allow God to reveal the true condition of our hearts and our Christian communities before him.

Introduction. The entire vision is too long for one study session, so only key passages are read and discussed. It would be helpful for you as a leader to read the entire passage (chaps. 8–11) as personal preparation for the study.

Question 1. Ezekiel is transported in this vision from the exile in Babylon to the temple complex in the heart of Jerusalem. He is then shown a series of vignettes revealing pagan practices in the temple itself: an idol image stood near the north gate (vv. 3, 5); the elders of Israel were secretly worshiping false gods and their images (vv. 11-12); a group of women were weeping for the arrival of Tammuz (a god of vegetation and fertility [v. 14]); and a cluster of twenty-five men worshiped the rising sun (v. 16). All these actions were forbidden by God in the strongest possible language, but here they were going on within the precincts of God's temple.

Question 2. You might need to ask additional questions to prompt discussion from the group. For example, we might not worship a visible idol of stone, but are there things that we put our trust or hope or security in other than God? Are there unhealthy or sinful habits (unclean creatures) that we have allowed to have a place in our lives? Are we wounded and upset (women weeping for a false god) when we lose money or possessions or when our pride is hurt? Do we strive for peace or fill the land with violence and hatred? What would our posts on social media reveal about us?

Question 3. These sins in public and in secret are met by God's anger (v. 18) and judgment. Continued disobedience will drive God's presence far from Israel's worship (v. 6). Even the people's cries for God's help will be ignored (v. 18). These severe judgments do not come after one sin but after a prolonged period of increasingly detestable actions. Read Jeremiah 7:9-10 for another prophet's perspective.

Question 4. Can we think that continued disobedience in our lives will bring any less severe consequences? These truths are not designed to drive us to despair but to push us toward repentance and the overflowing grace of God.

Question 5. This question should not be used to open the door to extreme criticism or bashing of an individual or a particular church. Instead, the focus should be on how we may be going through the motions of worship but with a heart far from God.

Question 7. The glory of the Lord moved from above the ark of the covenant in the most holy place of the temple to the threshold of the temple (v. 4). Then the glory of the Lord moved to the chariot throne of God (v. 18), which stood at the east entrance to the temple complex (v. 19). The final movement is from the east gate to the mountain east of Jerusalem (Ezekiel 11:23). The implication is that the glorious presence of God left the temple and the land and will not return until the glory returns to a new temple in a restored city (see Ezekiel 43:2; 44:2). The wavering of the glory (or the apparent movement back and forth) demonstrates the reluctance of the Lord to leave the temple and his people, but their sin is too great for him to remain.

Question 9. This question is not designed to open a door of criticism about the church but to prompt an honest evaluation of our sense and awareness of God's presence when we worship.

Question 10. God promises to give those he brings back to the land a new heart and a new spirit. This transformation will be accomplished by God's grace and power. Those who return will put away the abominations now present in the temple and the city. New hearts will produce new behavior. This is the same transformation that all human beings require—a radical change through salvation and an ongoing change as we are transformed in our behavior by God's Spirit day after day.

STUDY 5. TRAMPLING THE GRACE OF GOD. EZEKIEL 16:1-34, 59-63

PURPOSE: To search out and correct any elements of unfaithfulness in our lives and to learn to walk in purity before the Lord.

Introduction. In this chapter Ezekiel gives us a survey of Israel's spiritual history from its earliest origins to his own day. He embeds the account in the story of an abandoned child who is rescued by a traveler and eventually embraced as his wife. As Ezekiel tells it, however, it's not an endearing story. We feel repulsed by Ezekiel's realism, but Ezekiel meant to tell it that way. He was telling an ugly story of ugly sins, and he made the parable fit the facts. Ezekiel's "semipornographic style is a deliberate rhetorical device designed to produce a strong emotional response" (Daniel Block, *The Book of Ezekiel, Chapters 1-24*, New International Commentary on the Old Testament [Grand Rapids: Eerdmans, 1997], 467).

Question 1. Although the Lord addresses Jerusalem, the story applies to the whole nation of Israel. The nation was born in the land of the Canaanites. Abraham, Israel's physical father, lived in Canaan, and the tribes that descended from Abraham came back to Canaan after their slavery in Egypt. The Amorites and Hittites were pagan people who lived in Canaan before the people of Israel arrived. Remember that Ezekiel is not describing Israel's literal origin but its spiritual origins in the pagan culture of Canaan. The newborn child was unwanted, however, and was cast aside, unwashed and uncared for.

Question 2. The Lord "passed by" and chose to give life to the child, who would certainly have died without intervention. In the same way, we were spiritually lost and abandoned with no strength in ourselves to change our condition, and God in his grace chose to give us life. He provided all we needed to grow and flourish as we grew into maturity.

Question 4. God treated Israel with tender love and care. He met her needs and adorned her physically and spiritually. Under her husband's care and encouragement, Israel became a woman of beauty and strength. She was perfect "because [of] the splendor I had given you" (v. 14).

Question 5. Israel did not literally engage in sexual immorality with her idol-worshiping neighbors (although their rituals and idol worship often included immoral behavior). Instead Israel abandoned their covenant with the Lord in order to worship other gods. That false worship included making idols, sacrificing animals and even children to them, and giving offerings from the Lord's provision to these false gods. In addition, Israel's "lust" for pagan practices never seemed to be satisfied. Every new nation brought a new set of gods and new ways to heap insults on the true God.

Question 6. The people chose to forget God's grace in giving them life and providing them with his abundant blessings. They thought new gods and perverted worship would bring them happiness. We as Christians are certainly not to wallow in or be crushed by our past, but we can't forget our past either. We were lost and separated from God. But as far as sin had taken us, God in his grace was willing to rescue us. If we forget that, we can easily take a light view of sin and a casual view of grace.

Question 8. Israel's behavior went beyond the customary view of immorality and prostitution. While the prostitute engages in sexual activity for payment, Israel scorned payment (v. 31). Most prostitutes are solicited by men, but Israel did the soliciting and even paid the men to come to them (vv. 33-34). Israel was not just tempted into idolatry; she pursued it every chance she had.

Question 9. The point of this question is to raise the concern that when we willfully sin and pursue sinful behavior, we are violating our covenant with the Lord. It's a serious matter. We may mistakenly feel that we've merely broken some of God's rules and that the situation can be remedied easily. But sin is not just forgotten; sin must be forgiven, and that requires the payment of a price.

Question 10. The Lord makes it clear that punishment will certainly come on Israel (v. 59), but God's grace will ultimately overrule. God will remember his original covenant (his "wedding vows") and will enhance that covenant with "an everlasting covenant" (v. 60). Furthermore, God will make atonement for their sin (v. 63), setting him free to forgive them fully. When that covenant is made with Israel, the people will remember their past disobedience and be ashamed.

Question 12. God's love overcomes all our rebellion and all the obstacles we put in his way. He is relentless in his pursuit of those he loves. His love is totally undeserved. He loves because he chooses to love, not because something in those he loves is worthy or loveable. Ezekiel also emphasizes that God's love never changes. He may allow the consequences of our disobedience to come, but he never falters in his commitment to our good and his glory.

STUDY 6. THE LORD SEARCHES. EZEKIEL 22:1-31

PURPOSE: To challenge Christians to stand for truth and what is right in our culture—even if we stand alone.

Question 1. Every area of life is defiled by the people still living in Jerusalem. Their sins violate God's laws covering the protection of human life, parental authority, marriage, morality, property, and speaking the truth. The people exploit the weak and the vulnerable. You may want to use a white board to list all the sins drawn from this chapter by members of your group.

Question 3. God is quick to point out the people who are injured or hurt by the various leaders of Jerusalem. The foreigner, the fatherless, widows, older parents, the poor, the needy: all find themselves oppressed by the princes, priests, and politicians. The very people God wants his followers to care for and protect are targets of exploitation and attack. The purpose of the question about our contemporary society is not to spark a long debate about complex issues but to help group members see that some of the same oppression of the most vulnerable is still happening.

Question 4. We Christians may justify or ignore social violence or oppression or even participate in it in order to gain something for ourselves. God, however, still holds us accountable. "The over-all picture of extortion, bloodshed, immorality, incest, and irreligion is a terrifying description of any nation whose appointed time is drawing near" (John Taylor, *Ezekiel*, Tyndale Old Testament Commentaries [Downers Grove, IL: InterVarsity Press, 1969], 168).

Question 5. Israel's courage and self-justification will evaporate when they face God's judgment. God will then scatter them among the nations (v. 15). All who eventually stand before God for judgment will find no words to justify themselves. All that Christians have to cling to is the death and resurrection of Jesus on our behalf and in our place.

Question 6. God often uses the furnace of affliction and pain to pull from us those things that displease and dishonor him.

Question 8. In the heat of suffering or loss we find the marks of the old life being stripped off and the habits of the new life being put on. We emerge from a furnace experience purified and more willing to obey the Lord.

Question 9. Several key groups are singled out for rebuke: princes (v. 25), priests (v. 26), officials (v. 27), prophets (v. 28), and the common people (v. 29). God seems to hold rulers and spiritual leaders to a higher standard of obedience and spiritual integrity than he does the common people. The people follow the patterns set by the leaders.

Question 10. With that degree of corruption in Jerusalem's society, God looks for one person who will try to interpose himself to stop the nation's decline. This person's task is to stand before God in the broken places of society and to beg God to have mercy on his sinful people. This person is called to face the pain and risk that such prayer brings. Moses stood in the gap for Israel when they worshiped the golden calf (Psalm 106:23), but in Ezekiel's day no one was found. Therefore, judgment came.

STUDY 7. COUNTING THE COST. EZEKIEL 24:15-27

PURPOSE: To cause us to evaluate the cost of fully following the Lord.

Questions 1 and 2. God's word to Ezekiel must have sent a shock through the prophet. We know almost nothing about Ezekiel's wife except that she is "the delight of [his] eyes" (v. 16), indicating the level of intimacy between them. His shock is compounded by God's command not to mourn for her in the customary way. Some in your group may think God is being cruel to Ezekiel (or to his wife); some may feel upset that Ezekiel doesn't argue or bargain with God. Allow them to express their concerns or struggles. You don't have to give all the answers to such difficult questions.

Question 3 and 4. We never read of Ezekiel arguing with God. He seems to accept the Lord's authority without question. That is the challenge to us. Are we as willing to submit to the lordship of Christ and to accept whatever comes from his hand with the same faithful trust as Ezekiel displayed?

Question 5. "Here was a man, grasped by personal and human grief, who nevertheless saw beyond the immediacy of the moment to a greater grief that lay in store for all his people in the future. . . . Whatever the experience to which we are called in life, we need to remember that it may speak to others more coherently than any speech or sermon" (Peter Craigie, *Ezekiel*, Daily Study Bible [Louisville, KY: Westminster John Knox, 1983], 186-87). God allows Jerusalem to fall to a cruel Babylonian army—but God also holds the Babylonians accountable for their actions even though they are fulfilling God's judgment on his own people.

Question 6. God demonstrates grace to Ezekiel by allowing him to mourn privately. The normal mourning ritual for Ezekiel would have included loud crying, removing his priestly turban, and covering himself with rough sackcloth, dusted with ashes. When the exiles asked for an explanation of the prophet's lack of emotion, they received a declaration about what was happening in their native land.

Question 9. The people in exile would not only know that God knew about the fall of Jerusalem before it ever happened but also that he saw the events take place as the Babylonians destroyed the city. The Lord had repeatedly warned the people of the city's coming destruction and then had set events in motion to fulfill his predictions. God is sovereign not only in his knowledge of the future but also in bringing those events to pass.

Question 10. On the cross, God gave up his own beloved Son as the sacrifice for human sin. Before we knew or cared about Jesus, while we were still sinners, God the Father experienced the agony of seeing his Son tortured and killed (see Romans 5:6-8).

Question 11. These questions are designed to measure our obedience and loyalty against Ezekiel's commitment to the Lord. Would we willingly submit to God if the person or possession we loved most were taken from us?

The prayer suggestion can be used to draw the members of your group into a deeper sense of allegiance and submission to Jesus. The moment should not be rushed.

STUDY 8. RECEIVING A NEW HEART. EZEKIEL 36:16-38

PURPOSE: To understand what it means to be genuinely transformed by God.

Question 1. Once again Ezekiel expresses his contention that Israel's sins deserve God's judgment. The people have defiled the land and departed from the Lord. Because of this, God has scattered them among the nations. His act of judgment, however, has rebounded on his own good name and character. The nations were shocked that this would happen to the Lord's own people. It had made them think lightly of the God who had allowed his people to be treated like this.

Question 3 and 4. God acts for the sake of his holy character and reputation. God's love for Israel—and for us—is secondary to his holiness and his sovereign authority. Those aspects of God's character don't cancel each other out; they work together in perfect harmony. God's love for us flows from the satisfaction of his holy justice accomplished through the cross. Some of the things God does (or doesn't do) in our lives may stem from his concern for his own purpose and plan.

Question 5. God will vindicate himself and his promises to Israel not through continued suffering but through their restoration. Those who are scattered will be regathered (v. 24). God will sprinkle clean water on them to forgive their sins and to make them fit to enter his presence (v. 25). Beyond that, God will by his grace remove their unresponsive hearts of stone and give them a sensitive, responsive heart of flesh (v. 26). God will also put his own Spirit in them and guide them to joyful obedience (v. 27). The abundant blessing of prosperity in the land will be theirs to enjoy (vv. 28-30). In these verses all of the action is God's. Israel does not deserve God's blessing; they simply receive what grace offers.

Question 7. These verses seem out of place in Ezekiel's list of benefits, but we need to remember that God's actions emerge from his holy character, not from his desire to benefit his people. God's works are intended to display his glory to the world. Israel will be shamed by God's goodness in the light of their rebelliousness. We at times remember our former life or our deepest sins not to be overwhelmed by guilt but to be stirred to joy because we have been forgiven and welcomed into God's family.

Question 9. You may find differing opinions on this question. Some Christians believe that because of Israel's rejection of Jesus as their Messiah, God has rejected them and his promises to Israel are now fulfilled in his spiritual blessings to the church. Other Christians believe that, while God has set Israel aside temporarily, God will again focus on Israel in the future and will fulfill all his promises to them. Still others attribute all Old Testament promises to the future heavenly kingdom of God, where all of God's people from all ages will enjoy them together. The purpose of this question is not to spark intense debate but to get group members to think about God and his faithfulness to his promises.

Question 10. God is a covenant-keeping God, but he also expects faithfulness on the part of his people. He will respond but only when he hears "Israel's plea." Israel has to turn to the Lord in repentance and faith.

Question 11. Much of God's promise to Israel in this passage sounds like it comes from the New Testament! Under God's new covenant, which is secured by Jesus' death on the cross and his resurrection three days later, we are transformed inwardly by God's grace through God's Spirit. The images of prospering in the land can be taken as literal promises for a renewed nation of Israel (see question 5), but they can also be seen as spiritual promises to those who are in Christ. We are blessed abundantly with all spiritual blessings (see Ephesians 1:3). The images of prospering can also refer to God's future blessing to all his people during the reign of Christ on earth and on into eternity in the new earth we will inhabit (Revelation 21:1, 4).

Question 12. Often when we come to God for forgiveness, our focus is on our guilt and how badly we feel rather than on our insult to God's holy character. A proper understanding of the depth of God's grace and what was required to secure our cleansing and forgiveness will help us take a stand against sin in our lives.

STUDY 9. CAN THESE BONES LIVE? EZEKIEL 37:1-14

PURPOSE: To comprehend God's life-giving power to Israel and in our lives.

Question 1. Ezekiel saw this valley of bones in a vision. Two phrases in verse 1 seem to indicate that this was a spiritual experience in Ezekiel's life: "the hand of the LORD was on me" and "he brought me out by the Spirit."

Question 2. God wanted Ezekiel to see that these were all human bones, that there was a great number of them, and that they were very old. There was no possibility of a "survivor" among them. It was a scene of hopelessness that no human power could change. Any change to this scenario would require the power of God.

Question 3. The bones represented the nation of Israel—spiritually dead, physically scattered, beyond hope, and beyond help. The answer to God's question, "Can these bones live?" was only God knows.

Questions 4 and 5. God is not limited by what we perceive as impossible. Ezekiel has been promising the exiles a dramatic change in their circumstances:

new leaders, return to a restored land, rebuilt cities, and physical and spiritual abundance. His message was met with unbelief and mockery. The fall of Jerusalem would further erode the faith of the exiles. They looked at the situation in exile and at home and could only say, "Our bones are dried up and our hope is gone" (v. 11). Ezekiel, however, believed that renewal and restoration were possible. If God's purpose was to restore Israel, God would do it. God's Spirit has the power to turn scattered skeletons into an effective army bursting with life.

Question 6. God in his mercy and grace took those of us who were dead in sin, without hope or help, and by his power he gave us life and made us new. The work was by God's power alone, and the transformation was astonishing.

Question 7. Ezekiel was told to prophesy (the word can mean "preach" or "speak") to the bones (v. 4) and then to prophesy to the breath (the same Hebrew word translated "wind" and "Spirit") (v. 9). It must have seemed to Ezekiel like foolish things to do, but Ezekiel's life, as we have seen over and over, was marked by obedience. God accomplishes his purpose through the obedience of his people—usually through only one man or one woman!

Question 9. As Ezekiel preached to the bones, the effect was amazing but limited. The bones came together and were covered with flesh, but they were still dead. The second phase of the miracle was the Spirit's work of re-creation, to breathe physical and spiritual life into the reassembled bodies.

Question 10. This question allows for honest evaluation, but it should not be allowed to degenerate into criticism or blaming others. Instead focus on God's ability to bring renewal and revival into situations that seem hopeless to us.

Question 11. Ezekiel skillfully uses the Hebrew word *ruach* to refer to God's "Spirit" (vv. 1, 14), the "breath" that filled the lungs of the soldiers (vv. 5, 6, 8, 9, 10), and the "winds" that carried the life-giving air (v. 9). It is the same Hebrew word in each case. This is probably where Jesus drew the comparison between "wind" and "Spirit" during his conversation with Nicodemus in John 3:8: "The wind blows wherever it pleases. . . . So it is with everyone born of the Spirit."

People who are dead in sin may be alive physically but are unresponsive to God. They have no power in themselves to seek God or even to love God. Only the breath of God's Spirit enables those who are dead in sin to put their faith in Jesus. The Spirit draws us to Christ.

Questions 12 and 13. God can work in ways we don't expect or anticipate. We may write off a relationship or situation as hopeless, when in reality

God wants to work or is already at work to turn the situation around. He may be waiting to work until we take a step of obedience to something he has already said to us—forgive someone who has hurt us, humble ourselves to admit our part in the wrong, change an attitude or action in our life first, or give over a destructive habit to the Spirit's control.

STUDY 10. WORSHIP IN GOD'S NEW TEMPLE. EZEKIEL 43:1-12

PURPOSE: To examine the role of genuine worship today and in our future.

Question 1. The purpose of Ezekiel's final vision was more than just to give Israel a blueprint for a future temple. Just like in the tabernacle constructed in the wilderness and the first temple built by Solomon, the elements in this new temple would reflect something of the majesty and awesome character of the Lord. In this chapter, God's glory returns and fills the temple. It was a sign of God's acceptance of his people. He is willing to dwell with us and be close to us.

Question 2. When the glory departed from the temple just before Jerusalem was destroyed, it was because the temple was filled with idols and the people were following other gods. They weren't even aware that God's glorious presence was leaving. Now, however, the false cults and idols have been removed and put aside. And not only was the temple purified but also the people's hearts are made pure too.

Questions 3. Once again Ezekiel falls on his face in the presence of God (see Ezekiel 1:28). It was a sign of humility and absolute surrender. When we see Christ in his majesty and power and purity, we will not run up and shake his hand. We will fall before him in awe.

Question 4. We may experience a glimpse of that glory during our worship today, as a song of adoration is sung, as we bow before the Lord in prayer, as we behold the wonder of his creation, or witness a miracle of healing or restoration.

Questions 5. The Israelites in captivity already felt far from God's presence. They longed to worship again in God's temple in Jerusalem. They probably felt forgotten and hopeless with no way to change their situation. But God now tells them that he will come to them, where they are. God declares that he will dwell with them forever and never leave them.

Question 6. Those of us who live under the new covenant know the same personal intimacy with God. When Jesus came to earth as a human, God declared that Jesus was "God with us" (Matthew 1:23). Jesus also promised that he would be with us "always, to the very end of the age" (Matthew 28:20; see also Hebrews 13:5). Furthermore, those who have believed in Jesus are indwelt by the Holy Spirit (1 Corinthians 6:19), so we have God abiding in us, as close as a breath or a thought.

Question 7. Because the believer's body is the dwelling place of God's *Holy* Spirit, we are to treat our bodies as a sanctuary, a holy vessel for the Holy Spirit. That truth should affect what (and how much) we eat and drink, what substances we ingest, and how we treat (or neglect) our bodies. The discussion should not veer into legalism or judgment of each other, but it can be a profitable look at how we view and care for our bodies and why.

Question 8. The gathered community of believers is also a temple for the Spirit. Those around us in worship or in ministry are not just other people but living stones with us in the temple God lives in (1 Peter 2:5). We need to see them not as problems or obstacles, but as fellow members of God's family.

Douglas Connelly is a pastor, author, and speaker who lives in Davison, Michigan. He has written nineteen LifeGuide® Bible Studies for InterVarsity Press and is the author of The Bible Made Clear *and* The Book of Revelation Made Clear. *He and his wife, Karen, have three children and six grandchildren.*